ECONOMICS
OF THE
FUTURE

ECONOMICS
OF THE
FUTURE

A Compilation from the Bahá'í Writings

BADI SHAMS

BAHÁ'Í PUBLISHING TRUST

Bahá'í House, 6 Canning Road
New Delhi 110001, India

First Edition—1989
Second Edition—1991
Third Revised Edition—1998

ISBN : 81-85091-32-3

Printed at Nikhil Offset, 223, DSIDC Shed,
Okhla, Phase-I New Delhi-110020

PREFACE

The collection of writings for this compilation which started in 1979 was intended to be used for my research study on "Bahá'í Teachings on Economics". Teachings on this important subject are very scattered in the Bahá'í Writings. I have tried to classify them to the best of my ability, but I find the same very difficult since the guidelines given are very general and putting it under one heading, at times may not look justified.

The economic question in our time is a burning one and never a need for solving the economic problems of the world was felt as it is felt now.

No country belonging to any school of economic thought, whether developing or developed, can deny the fact that their main objective is to solve their economic problems.

There was never such a dire need for a better and deeper understanding of the teachings of the Bahá'í Faith on this subject, as more and more people now are eager to find out what solutions are found in the Bahá'í Writings.

It is hoped that after reading these wonderful writings on this subject you can analyse the current economic situation of the world and appreciate what the Bahá'í Faith has to offer.

I have to thank, the beloved Universal House of

Justice and their Research Department without whose help, guidance and corrections this compilation would have not been in existence.

—*Badi Shams*

CONTENTS

APPLICATION OF ECONOMIC
TEACHINGS TO MODERN PROBLEMS

"First we have to study the economic teachings in the light of modern problems more thoroughly so that we may advocate what the Founders of the Faith say and not what we conjecture from Their Writings. There is a great difference between sounding a great general principle and finding its application to actual prevailing conditions."

—*Shoghi Effendi, Directives from the Guardian, p. 20*

"For legal standards, political and economic theories are solely designed to safeguard the interests of humanity as a whole, and not humanity to be crucified for the preservation of the integrity of any particular law or doctrine."

—*Shoghi Effendi, The World Order of Bahá'u'lláh, p. 42*

"... The Teachings of Bahá'u'lláh and 'Abdu'l-Bahá do not provide specific and detailed solutions to all such economic questions which mostly pertain to the domain of *technical* economics, and as such do not concern *directly* the Cause. True, there are certain guiding principles in the Bahá'í Sacred Writings on the subject of economics, but these do by no means cover the whole field of theoretical and applied economics, and are mostly intended to guide future Bahá'í economic writers and technicians to evolve an economic system which would function in full conformity with the spirit, and the exact provisions of the Cause on this and similar subjects. The International House of Justice will have, in consultation with economic experts, to assist in the formulation and evolution of the Bahá'í economic system of the future. One thing however, is certain that the Cause neither accepts the theories of the Capitalistic economics *in full,* nor can it agree with the Marxists and Communists in their repudiation of the principle of private ownership and of the vital sacred rights of the individual."

—*From a letter written on behalf of Shoghi Effendi to an individual believer, June 10, 1930, Lights of Guidance*

"... the Writings are not so rich on this subject and many issues at present baffling the minds of the world are not even mentioned. The primary consideration is the Spirit that has to permeate our economic life and this will gradually crystallize·itself into definite institutions and principles that will help to bring about the ideal conditions foretold by Bahá'u'lláh."

—*From a letter, written on behalf of Shoghi Effendi to the National Spiritual Assembly of the United States and Canada, December 20, 1931: Bahá'í News, No. 90, March 1935, p. 2.*

AGRICULTURE AND FARMER

"... We must begin with the farmer, there will we lay a foundation for system and order because the peasant class and the agriculture class exceed other classes in the importance of their services."

—*'Abdu'l-Bahá, Star of the West, Vol. XIII, p. 228*

"The question of economics must commence with the farmer and therefore reach and· end with the other classes, inasmuch as the number of farmers is greater than all the classes, many many times greater. Therefore it is becoming that the economic problem be first solved with the farmer, for the farmer is the first active agent in the body politic. In brief, from among the wise men in every village a board should be organized and the affairs of that village be under the control of that board."

—*Extract from a Tablet of 'Abdu'l-Bahá, dated October 4, 1912, to an individual, sent by the Universal House of Justice to compiler.*

"Fifth: Complete regard should be had to the matter of agriculture. Although this matter is mentioned in the fifth, yet in reality it is endowed with the first station..."

—*Bahá'u'lláh, Tablet of the World, Bahá'í World Faith, p. 176*

"... of course conditions in the East differ where the Countries are rarely industrial and mostly agricultural we should have to apply different laws from the West and that is why the principles of the Movement strike at the root which is common to them both. 'Abdu'l-Bahá has developed in various of His talks, which you will find in different compilations, the principles upon which the Bahá'í economic system would be based. A system that prevents among others the gradual control of wealth in the hands of a few and the resulting state of both extremes, wealth and poverty."

—Shoghi Effendi, from a letter written on his behalf to an individual believer, October 28, 1927: Extracts from the Bahá'í Writings on the subject of Agriculture and Related Subjects, a compilation of the Universal House of Justice

"As to your fourth question, Shoghi Effendi believes that it is preferable not to confuse the methods explained by the Master with present systems. They may have many resemblances but also many points of difference. Moreover these general statements we have in the teachings have to be explained and applied by the House of Justice before we can really appreciate their significance."

—From a letter written on behalf of Shoghi Effendi to an individual believer, October 21, 1932, Lights of Guidance

BAHÁ'Í WORLD COMMONWEALTH

"... A single, organically-united, unshattered World Commonwealth."

—Shoghi Effendi, Messages to America, p. 81

"... a stage which, in the fullness of time, will culminate in the establishment of the World Bahá'í Commonwealth, functioning in the plenitude of its powers."

—Shoghi Effendi, Bahá'í World, Vol. XIII. p. 138

"... the precautionary and defensive measures to be devised, coordinated, and carried out to counteract the full force of the inescapable attacks which the organized efforts of ecclesiastical organizations of various denominations will progressively launch and relentlessly persue; and, last but not least, the multitudinous issues that must be faced, the obstacles that must be overcome, and the responsibilities that must be assumed, to enable a sore-tried Faith to pass through the successive stages of unmitigated obscurity, of active repression, and of complete emancipation, leading in turn to its being acknowledged as an independent Faith, enjoying the status of full equality with its sister religions, to be followed by its establishment and recognition as a State religion, which in turn must give way to its assumption of the rights and prerogatives associated with the Bahá'í state, functioning in the plenitude of its powers, a stage which must ultimately culminate in the emergence of the world-wide Bahá'í Commonwealth, animated wholly by the spirit, and operating solely in direct conformity with the laws and principles of Bahá'u'lláh."

—*Shoghi Effendi, The Advent of Divine Justice, p. 12*

"It is the structure of His New World Order, now stirring in the womb of the administrative institutions He Himself has created, that will serve both as a pattern and a nucleus of the World Commonwealth which is the sure, the inevitable destiny of the peoples and nations of the earth."

—*Shoghi Effendi, The Promised Day is Come, p. 122*

"It is the superstructure of that self-fame order, attaining its full stature through the emergence of the Bahá'í World Commonwealth—the Kingdom of God on earth—which the Golden Age of the (Bahá'í) Dispensation must, in the fullness of time, ultimately witness."

—*Shoghi Effendi, God Passes By, p. 26*

"As the authority with which Bahá'u'lláh has invested the future Bahá'í Commonwealth becomes more and more apparent, the fiercer shall be the challenge which from every quarter will be thrown at the verities it enshrines."

—*Shoghi Effendi, World Order of Bahá'u'lláh, p. 18*

"And as the Bahá'í Faith permeates the masses of the peoples of East and West, and its truth is embraced by the majority of the peoples of a number of the Sovereign States of the world, will the Universal House of Justice attain the plenitude of its power, and exercise, as the supreme organ of the Bahá'í Commonwealth, all the rights, the duties, and responsibilities incumbent upon the world's future superstate."

—*Shoghi Effendi, World Order of Bahá'u'lláh, p. 7*

"Haifa, Israel—'permanent world Administrative Centre of the future Bahá'í Commonwealth, destined never to be separated from, and to function in proximity of the Spiritual Centre of (the) Faith' ..."

—*Shoghi Effendi, God Passes By, p. 348*

"... To us, the 'generation of the half-light', living at a time which may be designated as the period of the incubation of the World Commonwealth envisaged by Bahá'u'lláh, has been assigned a task whose high privilege we can never sufficiently appreciate, and the arduousness of which we can as yet but dimly recognize."

—*Shoghi Effendi, World Order of Bahá'u'lláh, p. 168*

"... the Faith of Bahá'u'lláh now visibly succeeding in demonstrating its claim and title to be regarded as a World Religion destined to attain, in the fullness of time, the status of a world-embracing Commonwealth, which would be at once the instrument and the guardian of the Most Great peace, announced by its Author."

—*Shoghi Effendi, World Order of Bahá'u'lláh, p. 196*

"The process of disintegration must inexorably continue, and its corrosive influence must penetrate deeper and deeper into the very core of a crumbling age. Much suffering will still be required ere the contending nations, creeds, classes and races of mankind are fused in the crucible of universal affliction, and are forged by the fires of a fierce ordeal into one organic commonwealth, one vast, unified and harmoniously functioning system. Adversities unimaginably appalling, undreamed of crises and up-heavals, war, famine and pestilence, might well combine to engrave in the soul of an unheeding generation those truths and principles which it has disdained to recognize and follow."

—*Shoghi Effendi, World Order of Bahá'u'lláh, p. 193*

"The Declaration of Trust and By-Laws of the National Spiritual Assembly of the United States, stands in its final form as a worthy and faithful exposition of the constitutional basis of the Bahá'í communities in every land, foreshadowing the final emergence of the World Bahá'í Commonwealth of the future."

—*Shoghi Effendi, Bahá'í Administration, p. 135*

"This final and crowning stage (Commonwealth)

in the evolution of the Plan wrought by God Himself
for humanity will, in turn, prove to be the signal for
the birth of a world civilization, incomparable in its
range, its character and potency, in the history of
mankind..."

—*Shoghi Effendi, Bahá'í World, Vol. XI, p. 138*

BAHÁ'Í ECONOMIC SYSTEM

"There are practically no technical teachings on
economics in the Cause, such as banking, the price
system, and others. The Cause is not an economic
system, nor can its Founders be considered as
having been technical economists. The contribution of
the Faith to this subject is essentially indirect, as it
consists of the application of spiritual principles to
our present-day economic system. Bahá'u'lláh has
given us a few basic principles which should guide
future Bahá'í economists in establishing such
institutions as will adjust the economic relationships
of the world."

—*Shoghi Effendi, Principles of Bahá'í Administration, pp. 27-28*

"With regard to your wish for reorganizing your
business along Bahá'í lines, Shoghi Effendi deeply
appreciates the spirit that has prompted you to
make such a suggestion. But he feels nevertheless
that the time has not yet come for any believer to
bring about such a fundamental change in the
economic structure of our society, however restricted
may be the field for such an experiment. The
economic teachings of the Cause, though well known
in their main outline, have not as yet been sufficiently

elaborated and systematized to allow anyone to make an exact and thorough application of them even on a restricted scale."

—*Letter written on behalf of Shoghi Effendi by his secretary, Principles of Bahá'í Administration, p. 28*

"The International House of Justice will have, in consultation with economic experts, to assist in the formulation and evolution of the Bahá'í economic system of the future."

—*Shoghi Effendi, letter on his behalf to an individual believer, June 10, 1939, Lights of Guidance*

"... the Writings are not so rich on this subject and many issues at present baffling the minds of the world are not even mentioned. The primary consideration is the spirit that has to permeate our economic life, and this will gradually crystallize itself into definite institutions and principles that will help to bring about the ideal condition foretold by Bahá'u'lláh."

—*Shoghi Effendi, Directives from the Guardian, p. 19*

"No, Bahá'u'lláh did not bring a complete system of economics to the world. Profit sharing is recommended as a solution to one form of Economic Problems."

—*Shoghi Effendi, Directives from the Guardian, p. 19*

"As regards the activities of the Economic Committee of the National Assembly; Shoghi Effendi fully sympathizes with the desire of some of the members to see the Committee find ways and means to put into practice the economic teachings of the Cause, as explained in some of the recorded Writings and Sayings of Bahá'u'lláh and the Master.

But he believes that the time is not yet ripe for such activities."

—*Shoghi Effendi, Directives from the Guardian, p. 20*

BENEVOLENCE—
GREATER THAN EQUALITY

"...In the Teachings of Bahá'u'lláh benevolence (is enjoined) and this is greater than equality. Equality is attained through force, but benevolence is a voluntary act (or is a matter of choice). Man's perfection is achieved through good deeds done voluntarily, not by good deeds done through compulsion, and benevolence is a good deed performed voluntarily. That means that the rich should be benevolent towards the poor—that is, give to the poor, but by their own free will and desire—not that the poor should compel the rich to do so. For compulsion breeds discord, and disrupts the order in human affairs. For benevolence, which is voluntary benefaction, engenders peacefulness in the world of humanity, and it brings illumination to the realm of man."

—*Tablet of 'Abdu'l-Bahá to Andrew Carnegie, published in World Order magazine January 1949— This Tablet was translated by Mírzá-'Alí-Kulí Khán*

"And among the teachings of Bahá'u'lláh is voluntary sharing of one's property with others among mankind. This voluntary sharing is greater than equality, and consists in this: That man should not prefer himself to others, but rather should sacrifice his life and property for others. But this should not be introduced by coercion so that it becomes a law and man is compelled to follow it."

—*'Abdu'l-Bahá, Foundations of World Unity, p. 30*

CAPITALIST AND CAPITALISM

"If it be right for a capitalist to possess a large fortune, it is equally just that his workman should have a sufficient means of existence."

—*'Abdu'l-Bahá, Paris Talks, p. 153*

"It lies in the capitalists being moderate in the acquisition of their profits, and in their having a consideration for the welfare of the poor and needy, that is to say, that the workmen and artisans receive a fixed and established daily wage, and have a share in the general profits of the factory."

—*'Abdu'l-Bahá, Some Answered Questions, p. 316*

"There is nothing in the teachings against some kind of capitalism, its present form, though, would require adjustments to be made."

—*Shoghi Effendi, Directives from the Guardian, p. 19*

CHARITY AND ENDOWMENT

"This Bahá'í teaching of human fellowship and kindness implies that we must be always ready to extend every assistance and help we can to those who are in distress and suffering. Bahá'í charity is of the very essence of the Teachings, and should therefore be developed in every Bahá'í community. Charitable institutions such as orphanages, free schools and hospitals for the poor, constitute an indispensable part of the Mashriqu'l-Adhkár. It is the responsibility of every local Bahá'í community to insure the welfare of its poor and needy members, through whatever means possible.

"But, of course, this extension of assistance to the poor, in whatever form, should under no circumstances be allowed to seriously interfere with the major collective interests of the Bahá'í community, as distinguished from the purely personal interests of its members. The demands of the Cause transcend those of the individual, and should therefore be given precedence. But these two phases of Bahá'í social life, though not of equal importance, are by no means contradictory. Both of them are essential, and should be fostered, but each according to its own degree of importance. It is the responsibility of Baha'í assemblies to decide when individual interest should be subordinated to those affecting the collective welfare of the community. But, as already stated, the interests of the individual should always be safeguarded within certain limits, and provided they do not seriously affect the welfare of the group as a whole."

—*Shoghi Effendi, letter written on his behalf to an individual
believer, June 26, 1936*

"Charity is pleasing and praiseworthy in the sight of God and is regarded as a prince among goodly deeds. Consider ye and call to mind that which the All-Merciful hath revealed in the Qur'án: They prefer them before themselves, though poverty be their own lot. And with such as are preserved from their own convetousness shall it be well,' (Qur'án 59:9) Viewed in this light, the blessed utterance above is, in truth, the day-star of utterances. Blessed is he who preferreth his brother before himself. Verily, such a man is reckoned, by virtue of the Will of God, the All-Knowing, the All-Wise, with the people of Bahá who dwell in the Crimson Ark."

—*Bahá'u'lláh, Words of Paradise, Writings of Bahá'u'lláh, p. 205*

"It is not necessary to undertake special journeys to visit the resting-places of the dead. If people of substance and affluence offer the cost of such journeys to the House of Justice, it will be pleasing and acceptable in the presence of God. Happy are they that observe His precepts."

—*Bahá'u'lláh, The fourteenth Glad-Tidings,*
Writings of Bahá'u'lláh, p. 184

"Fourth: Everyone, whether man or woman, should hand over to a trusted person a portion of what he or she earneth through trade, agriculture or other occupation, for the training and education of children, to be spent for this purpose with the knowledge of the Trustees of the House of Justice."

—*Bahá'u'lláh, Tablet of the World, Writings of Bahá'u'lláh,*
p. 214-215

COMPETITION

"In the world of nature the greatest dominant note is the struggle for existence—the result of which

is the survival of the fittest. The law of the survival
of the fittest is the origin of all difficulties. It is the
cause of war and strife, hatred and animosity
between human beings."

—*'Abdu'l-Bahá, Star of the West, Vol, VIII, p. 15*

"Shall he then remain its captive, even failing to
qualify under the natural law which commands the
survival of the fittest. That is to say shall he continue
to live upon the level of the animal kingdom without
distinction between them and himself in natural
impulses and ferocious instincts?"

—*'Abdu'l-Bahá, The Promulgation of Universal Peace, p. 353*

"In nature there is the law of the survival of the
fittest. Even if man be not educated, then according
to the natural institutes this natural law will demand
of man supremacy. The purpose and object of
schools, colleges and universities is to educate man
and thereby rescue and redeem him from the
exigencies and defects of nature and to awaken
within him the capability of controlling and
appropriating nature's bounties."

—*'Abdu'l-Bahá, The Promulgation of Universal Peace, p. 353*

DIVINE ECONOMY

"... does not the very operation of the... forces
that are at work in this age necessitate that... the
Bearer of the Message of God... should embody... the
essentials of that social code, that Divine Economy,
which must guide humanity's concerted efforts in

establishing that all embracing federation which is to signalize the advent of the Kingdom of God on this earth?"

—*Shoghi Effendi, The World Order of Bahá'u'lláh, p. 61*

"In like manner are the Bahá'í economic principles the embodiment of the highest aspirations of all wage-earning classes and of economists of various schools."

—*'Abdu'l-Bahá, Tablet to Dr. Auguste Forel, dated 21 September, 1921, Auguste Forel and the Bahá'í Faith, p. 26*

"... By the statement the economic solution is Divine in nature' is meant that religion alone can, in the last resort, bring in man's nature such a fundamental change as to enable him to adjust the economic relationships of society. It is only in this way that man can control the economic forces that threaten to disrupt the foundations of his existence, and thus assert his mastery over the forces of nature."

—*From a letter written on behalf of Shoghi Effendi to an individual believer, December 26, 1935, Lights of Guidance*

DIFFERENT DEGREES AND CAPACITIES OF MAN

"Nevertheless, there will be preservation of degrees because in the world of humanity there must needs be degrees. The body politic may well be likened to an army. In this army there must be a general, there must be a sergeant, there must be a marshal, there must be the infantry; but all must enjoy the greatest comfort and welfare."

—*'Abdu'l-Bahá, Star of the West, Vol. XIII, p. 229*

"The arrangements of the circumstances of the people must be such that poverty shall disappear, that everyone, as far as possible, according to his rank and position, shall share in comfort and well-being.

"We see amongst us men who are overburdened with riches on the one hand, and on the other those unfortunate ones who starve with nothing; those who possess several stately palaces, and those who have not where to lay their head. Some we find with numerous courses of costly and dainty food; whilst others can scarce find sufficient crusts to keep them alive. Whilst some are clothed in velvets, furs and fine lines, others have insufficient, poor and thin garments with which to protect them from the cold."

—*'Abdu'l-Bahá, Paris Talks, p. 151*

"Some are full of intelligence, others have an ordinary amount of it, and others again are devoid of intellect. In these three classes of men there is order but not equality. How could it be possible that wisdom and stupidity should be equal? Humanity, like a great army, requires a general, captains, under-officers in their degree, and soldiers, each with their own appointed duties. Degrees are absolutely necessary to ensure an orderly organization. An army could not be composed of generals alone, or of captains only, or of nothing but soldiers without one in authority. The certain result of such a plan would be that disorder and demoralization would overtake the whole army."

—*'Abdu'l-Bahá, Paris Talks, p. 152*

"The essence of the matter is that Divine Justice will become manifest in human conditions and affairs, and all mankind will find comfort and enjoyment in life. It is not meant that all will be equal, for inequality in degree and capacity is a property of nature. Necessarily there will be rich people and also those who will be in want of their livelihood, but in the aggregate community there will be equalization and re-adjustment of values and interests."

—*'Abdu'l-Bahá, The Promulgation of Universal Peace, p. 132*

"For the community needs financier, farmer, merchant and labourer just as an army must be composed of commander, officers and privates. All cannot be commanders; all cannot be officers or privates. Each in his station in the social fabric must be competent; each in his function according to ability; but justness of opportunity for all."

—*'Abdu'l-Bahá, The Promulgation of Universal Peace, p. 216*

"When the laws He has instituted, are carried out, there will be no millionaires possible in the community and likewise no extremely poor. This will be effected and regulated by adjusting the different degrees of human capacity."

—*'Abdu'l-Bahá, The Promulgation of Universal Peace, p. 217*

"Social inequality is the inevitable outcome of the natural inequality of man. Human beings are different in ability and should, therefore, be different in their social and economic standing."

—*Shoghi Effendi, Directives from the Guardian, p. 20*

DIVINE CIVILIZATION

"Material civilization has reached an advanced plane but now there is need of spiritual civilization. Material civilization alone will not satisfy; it cannot meet the conditions and requirements of the present age. Its benefits are limited to the world of matter. There is no limitation to the spirit of man, for spirit in itself is progressive and if the divine civilization be established the spirit of man will advance."

—*'Abdu'l-Bahá, The Promulgation of Universal Peace, p. 101*

"Every developed susceptibility will increase the effectiveness of man. Discoveries of the real will become more and more possible and the influence of divine guidance will be increasingly recognized. All this is conducive to the divine form of civilization... The capacity of human kind will be tested and a degree shall be attained where equality is a reality."

—*'Abdu'l-Bahá, The Promulgation of Universal Peace, p. 101*

"As heretofore material civilization has been extended, the divine civilization must now be promulgated. Until the two agree, real happiness among mankind will be unknown. By mere intellectual development and power of reason, man cannot attain to his fullest degree; that is to say, by means of intellect alone he cannot accomplish the progress effected by religion."

—*'Abdu'l-Bahá, The Promulgation of Universal Peace, p. 170*

"While it is true that its people (America) have attained a marvellous material civilization, I hope that spiritual forces may animate this great body."

—*'Abdu'l-Bahá, The Promulgation of Universal Peace, p. 20*

"And among the Teachings of Bahá'u'lláh is that although material civilization is one of the means for progress of the world of mankind, yet until it becomes combined with divine civilization the desired result, which is the felicity of mankind, will not be attained."

—*'Abdu'l-Bahá, Foundations of World Unity, p. 30*

"Material civilization is like a globe of glass. Divine civilization is the light itself, and the glass without the light is dark. Material civilization is like the body. No matter how infinitely graceful, elegant and beautiful it may be, it is dead. Divine civilization is like the spirit, and the body gets its life from the spirit, otherwise it becomes a corpse. It has thus been made evident that the world of mankind is in need of the breaths of the Holy Spirit."

—*'Abdu'l-Bahá, Foundations of World Unity, p. 31*

DETACHMENT

"Cast away that which ye possess, and, on the wings of detachment, soar beyond all created things. Thus biddeth you the Lord of Creation, the movement of Whose pen hath revolutionized the soul of mankind."

—*Synopsis and Codification of the Kitáb-i-Aqdas, p. 16*

"What advantage is there in the earthly things which men possess? That which shall profit them, they have utterly neglected."

—*Synopsis and Codification of the Kitáb-i-Aqdas, p. 16*

"O MY SERVANT !

Free thyself from the fetters of this world, and loose the Soul from the prison of self. Seize thy chance, for it will come to thee no more."

—*Bahá'u'lláh, The Hidden Words, from the Persian, No. 40*

"O SON OF PASSION !

Cleanse thyself from the defilement of riches and in perfect peace advance into the realm of poverty; that from the well-spring of detachment thou mayest quaff the wine of immortal life."

—*Bahá'u'lláh, The Hidden Words, from the Persian, No. 55*

"... Earthly treasures. We have not bequeathed, nor have We added such cares as they entail. By God! In earthly riches fear is hidden and peril is concealed. Consider ye and call to mind that which the All-Merciful hath revealed in the Qur'án: 'Woe betide every slanderer and defamer, him that layeth up riches and counteth them.' (*Qur'án 104:1-2*) Fleeting are the riches of the world; all that perisheth and changeth is not, and hath never been, worthy of attention, except to a recognized measure..."

—*Bahá'u'lláh, Kitáb-i-'Ahd (Book of the Covenant),
Writings of Bahá'u'lláh, p. 278*

ECONOMIC RESOURCES

"... The economic resources of the world will be organised, its sources of raw materials will be tapped and fully utilized, its markets will be co-ordinated and developed, and the distribution of its products will be equitably regulated.

"... The enormous energy dissipated and wasted on war, whether economic or political, will be consecrated to such ends as will extend the range of human inventions and technical development, to the increase of the productivity of mankind, to the extermination of disease, to the extension of scientific research, to the raising of the standard of physical health, to the sharpening and refinement of the human brain, to the exploitation of the unused and unsuspected resources of the planet, to the prolongation of human life, and to the furtherance of any other agency that can stimulate the intellectual, the moral, and spiritual life of the entire human race. A world federal system, ruling the whole earth and exercising unchallengeable authority over its unimaginably vast resources, blending and embodying the ideals of both the East and the West, liberated from the curse of war and its miseries, and bent on the exploitation of all the available sources of energy on the surface of the planet, a system in which Force is made the servant of Justice, whose life is sustained by its universal recognition of one God and by its allegiance to one common Revelation—such is the goal towards which humanity, impelled by the unifying forces of life, is moving..."

—*Shoghi Effendi, The World Order of Bahá'u'lláh, p. 204*

"Praise be to God: A wonderful thing is perceived; the lightning and similar forces are subdued by a Conductor, and act by His Command. O People of Bahá! Each one of the revealed Commands is a strong fortress for the protection of the world."

—*Bahá'u'lláh, Bahá'í World Faith, p. 183*

"From every standpoint the world of humanity is undergoing a re-formation... scientific ideas and theories are developing and advancing to meet a new range of phenomena, invention and discovery are penetrating hitherto unknown fields revealing new wonders and hidden secrets of the material universe. Industries have vastly wider scope and production; everywhere the world of mankind is the theories of evolutionary activity indicating the passing of the old conditions and advent of the New Age of reformation."

—*'Abdu'l-Bahá, Foundations of World Unity, p. 10*

ECONOMIC RE-ADJUSTMENT

"The fourth Principle or Teaching of Bahá'u'lláh is the re-adjustment and equalization of the economic standards of mankind. This deals with the question of human livelihood. It is evident that under present systems and conditions of government the poor are subject to the greatest need and distress while others more fortunate live in luxury and plenty far beyond their actual necessities."

—*'Abdu'l-Bahá, The Promulgation of Universal Peace, p. 107*

"... Through the Manifestation of God's great equity the poor of the world will be rewarded and assisted fully and there will be a re-adjustment in the economic conditions of mankind so that in the future there will not be the abnormally rich nor the abject poor."

—*'Abdu'l-Bahá, The Promulgation of Universal Peace, p. 132*

"The re-adjustment of the economic laws for the livelihood of man must be effected in order that all humanity may live in the greatest happiness according to their respective degrees."

—*'Abdu'l-Bahá, The Promulgation of Universal Peace, p. 170*

"... This re-adjustment of the social economy is of the greatest importance inasmuch as it ensures the stability of the world of humanity; and until it is effected, happiness and prosperity are impossible."

—*'Abdu'l-Bahá, The Promulgation of Universal Peace, p. 181*

ECONOMIC PROBLEMS

Nature and Causes of Economic Problems

"It seems as though all creatures can exist singly and alone. For example, a tree can exist solitary and alone on a given prairie or in a valley or on the mountain side. An animal upon a mountain or a bird soaring in the air might live a solitary life. They are not in need of co-operation or solidarity. Such animated beings enjoy the greatest comfort and happiness in their respective solitary lives.

"On the contrary, man cannot live singly and alone. He is in need of continuous co-operation and mutual help.

"For example, a man living alone in the wilderness will eventually starve. He can never, singly and alone, provide himself with all the necessities of existence. Therefore, he is in need of co-operation and reciprocity.

"Although the body politic is one family yet because of lack of harmonious relations some members are comfortable and some in direst misery, some members are satisfied and some are hungry, some members are clothed in most costly garments and some families are in need of food and shelter. Why? Because this family lacks the necessary reciprocity and symmetry. This household is not well arranged. This household is not living under a perfect law. All the laws which are legislated do not ensure happiness. They do not provide comfort. Therefore a law must be given to this family by means of which all the members of this family will enjoy equal well-being and happiness. Is it possible for one member of a family to be subjected to the utmost misery and to abject poverty and for the rest of the family to be comfortable? It is impossible unless those members of the family be senseless, atrophied, inhospitable, unkind.

"Such utter indifference in the human family is due to *lack of control, to lack of a working law, to lack of kindness* in its midst. If kindness had been shown to the members of this family surely all the members thereof would have enjoyed comfort and happiness."

—*'Abdu'l-Bahá, Star of the West, Vol. XIII, pp. 227-228*

"But the principal cause of these difficulties lies in the laws of the present civilization; for they lead to a small number of individuals accumulating incomparable fortunes, beyond their needs, whilst the greater number remains destitute, stripped and in the

greatest misery..."
—'Abdu'l-Bahá, *Some Answered Questions, p. 313*

"The body of the human world is sick. Its remedy and healing will be the oneness of the kingdom of humanity. Its life is the 'Most Great Peace'. Its illumination and quickening is love."
—'Abdu'l-Bahá, *The Promulgation of Universal Peace, p. 19*

"Economic plans of reconstruction have been carefully devised, and meticulously executed. And yet crisis has succeeded crisis, and the rapidity with which a perilously unstable world is declining has been correspondingly accelerated. A yawning gulf threatens to involve in one common disaster both the satisfied and dissatisfied nations, democracies and dictatorships, capitalists and wage-earners, Europeans and Asiatics, Jew and Gentile, white and coloured."
—Shoghi Effendi, *The World Order of Bahá'u'lláh, p. 190*

Solution to Economic Problems

"The secrets of the whole economic question are Divine in nature, and are concerned with the world of the heart and spirit. In the Bahá'í Teachings this is most completely explained, and without the consideration of the Bahá'í Teachings, it is impossible to bring about a better state."
—'Abdu'l-Bahá, *The Bahá'í World, Vol. IV. p. 448*

"The Bahá'í Cause covers all economic and social questions under the heading and ruling of its laws. The essence of the Bahá'í spirit is that in order to establish a better social order and economic condition, there must be allegiance to the laws and principles of government."

—*'Abdu'l-Bahá, The Promulgation of Universal Peace, p. 238*

"All economic problems may be solved by the application of the science of the Love of God."

—*'Abdu'l-Bahá, Portals to Freedom, p. 156*

"... 'All economic problems may be solved by the application of the Science of the Love of God.' That is to say: If the Rule called golden and treated as if it were leaden (Worse: For lead has its uses but so far as one may determine, the Golden Rule has been laid on a shelf whose dust is seldom disturbed)—if that Rule were actually applied to the world's economic problems, which if not solved bid fair to destroy us, and the love of God, the sort of love which makes a home life happy, were used *as a scientific* measurement to regulate our international and national affairs; to settle all relations between labour and capital, between rich and poor, to regulate all coinage and commerce, can there be any doubt that the results would be far more conducive to human welfare than our present policies have produced?"

—*'Abdu'l-Bahá, Portals to Freedom, p. 156*

EQUALITY

"O CHILDREN OF MEN !

Know ye not why We created you all from the same dust? That no one should exalt himself over the other. Ponder at all times in your hearts how ye were created. Since We have created you all from one same substance it is incumbent on you to be even as one soul, to walk with the same feet, eat with the same mouth and dwell in the same land, that from your inmost being, by your deeds and actions, the signs of oneness and the essence of detachment may be made manifest. Such is My counsel to you, O concourse of light! Heed ye this counsel that ye may obtain the fruit of holiness from the tree of wonderous glory."

—*Bahá'u'lláh, The Hidden Words, from the Arabic, No. 68*

"Likewise with regard to the party of 'equality' which seeks the solution of the economic problems: Until now all proposed solutions have proved impracticable except the economic proposals in the Teachings of His Holiness Bahá'u'lláh, which are practicable and cause no distress to society."

—*'Abdu'l-Bahá, Foundations of World Unity, p. 32*

"But in the Divine Teachings equality is brought about through a ready willingness to share. It is commanded as regards wealth that the rich among the people, and the aristocrats should, by their own free will and for the sake of their own happiness, concern themselves with and care for the poor. This equality is the result of the lofty characteristics and noble attributes of mankind."

—*'Abdu'l-Bahá, Tablet of Olly Schwarz, Stuttgart, February 1920,*
Star of the West, Vol. XIII. p. 231

"Now the remedy must be carefully undertaken. It cannot be done by bringing to pass absolute equality between men.

"Equality is a chimera! It is entirely impracticable! Even if equality could be achieved it could not continue—and if its existence were possible, the whole order of the world would be destroyed. The law of order must always obtain in the world of humanity. Heaven has so decreed in the creation of man."

—*'Abdu'l-Bahá, Paris Talks, pp, 151-152*

"Thus, there is a great wisdom in the fact that equality is not imposed by law: It is, therefore, preferable for moderation to do its work. The main point is, by means of laws and regulations to hinder the constitution of the excessive fortunes of certain individuals, and to protect the essential needs of the masses. For instance, the manufacturers and the industrials heap up a treasure each day, and the poor artisans do not gain their daily sustenance: that is the height of iniquity, and no just man can accept it."

—*'Abdu'l-Bahá, Some Answered Questions, pp. 314-315*

GREAT DEPRESSION

"The Great Depression, the aftermath of the severest ordeals humanity had ever experienced, the aftermath of the Versailles system, the recrudescene of militarism in its most menacing aspects, the failure of vast experiments and new-born institutions to safeguard the peace and tranquillity of peoples, classes and nations, have bitterly disillusioned humanity and prostrated its spirits."

—*Shoghi Effendi, The World Order of Bahá'u'lláh, p. 188*

ḤUQÚQU'LLÁH

"Upon thee be My glory and My loving-kindness. Nothing that existeth in the world of being hath ever been or ever will be worthy of mention. However, if a person be graciously favoured to offer a penny-worth-nay even less-in the path of God, this would in His sight be preferable and superior to all the treasures of the earth. It is for this reason that the one true God—exalted be His glory—hath in all His heavenly Scriptures praised those who observe His precepts and bestow their wealth for His sake. Beseech ye God that He may enable everyone to discharge the obligation of Ḥuqúq, inasmuch as the progress and promotion of the Casue of God depend on material means. If His faithful servants could realize how meritorious are benevolent deeds in these days, they would all arise to do that which is meet and seemly. In His hand is the source of authority and He ordaineth as He willeth. He is the Supreme Ruler, the Bountiful, the Equitable, the Revealer, the All-Wise."

—Bahá'u'lláh, Compilation on Huqúqu'lláh, p.1

"It is incumbent upon everyone to discharge the obligation of Ḥuqúq. The advantages gained from this deed revert to the persons themselves. However the acceptance of the offerings dependeth on the spirit of joy, fellowship and contentment that the righteous souls who fulfil this injunction will manifest. If such is the attitude acceptance is permissible and not otherwise. Verily thy Lord is the All-Sufficing, the All-Praised."

—Bahá'u'lláh, Compilation on Huqúqu'lláh, p.3

"Ḥuqúqu'lláh is indeed a great law. It is incumbent upon all to make this offering, because it is the source of grace, abundance, and of all good. It is a bounty which shall remain with every soul in every world of the worlds of God, the All-Possessing, the All-Bountiful."

—*Bahá'u'lláh, Compilation on Ḥuqúqu'lláh, p.4*

"... May my Glory rest upon thee! Fix thy gaze upon the glory of the Cause. Speak forth that which will attract the hearts and the minds. To demand the Ḥuqúq is in no wise permissible. This command was revealed in the Book of God for various necessary matters ordained by God to be dependent upon material means. Therefore, if someone, with utmost pleasure and gladness, nay with insistence, wisheth to partake of this blessing, thou mayest accept. Otherwise, acceptance is not permissible."

—*Bahá'u'lláh, Compilation on Huqúqu'lláh, p.5*

"Question : It hath been revealed in the Divine Tablets that if a person acquireth the equivalent of nineteen mithqáls of gold, he must pay the Right of God on that sum. How much of that sum shall be paid:

"Answer : God hath commanded that nineteen be paid out of every hundred. This should be the basis of computation. The sum due on nineteen can then be determined."

—*Bahá'u'lláh, Compilation on Ḥuqúqu'lláh, p.8*

"The minimum amount subject to Huqúqu'lláh is reached when one's possessions are worth the number of Váḥid (19); that is, whenever one owneth 19 mithqáls of gold, or acquireth possessions attaining this value, after having deducted therefrom the yearly expenses, the Ḥuqúq becometh applicable and its payment is obligatory."

—*Bahá'u'lláh, Compilation on Ḥuqúqu'lláh, p.9*

"According to that which is revealed in the Most Holy Book. Ḥuqúqu'lláh is fixed at the rate of 19 miṯẖqáls out of every 100 miṯẖqáls worth of gold. This applies to possessions in gold, in silver or other properties.

"Moreover certain rights have been fixed for the House of Justice. However before its establishment and the appearance of its members, the appropriation of such funds is and will be subject to the approval of Him Who is the Eternal Truth. Beseech ye God—exalted be His Glory—to enable the people to honour the obligation of Huqúq, for had everyone perceived the advantage of such a deed and desisted from with-holding the Right of God, the friends in that region would not have experienced any hardship."

—*Bahá'u'lláh, Compilation on Ḥuququ'lláh, p.10*

"Thine intention to pay a visit to the blessed House is acceptable and well-pleasing in the sight of this Wronged One, provided it is accomplished in a spirit of joy and radiance and would not prove contrary to the dictates of wisdom.

"Say : O people, the first duty is to recognize the one true God—magnified be His Glory—the second is to show forth constancy in His Cause and, after these, one's duty is to purify one's riches and earthly possessions according to that which is prescribed by God. Therefore it beseemeth thee to meet thine obligation to the Right of God first, then to direct thy steps toward His blessed House. This hath been brought to thine attention as a sign of favour."

—*Bahá'u'lláh, Compilation on Ḥuqúqu'lláh, p.18*

"Payments for the Ḥuqúqu'lláh cannot be handed over to every person. These words have been uttered by Him Who is the sovereign Truth. The Ḥuqúqu'lláh should be kept in the custody of trusted individuals and forwarded to His holy court through the Trustees of God."

—*Bahá'u'lláh, Compilation on Ḥuqúqu'lláh, p.33*

"Thou hast enquired about the Ḥuqúq. From one's annual income, all expenses during the year are deductible, and on what is left 19% is payable to the Ḥuqúq. Thus, a person hath earned £1000 income out of his business. After deducting his annual expenses of say £600, he would have surplus of £400 on which Ḥuqúq is payable at the rate of 19%. This would amount to £76 to be offered for charitable purposes to the Ḥuqúq.

"The Ḥuqúq is not levied on one's entire possessions each year. A person's wealth may be worth £100,000. How can be he expected to pay Ḥuqúq on this property every year? For instance, whatever income thou hast earned in a particular year, you should deduct from it your expenses during that year. The Ḥuqúq will then be payable on the remainder. Possessions on which Ḥuqúq was paid the previous year will be exempt from further payment."

—*'Abdu'l-Bahá, Compilation on Ḥuqúqu'lláh, p.40*

"Ḥuqúq is applied on everything one possesseth.

However, if a person hath paid the Ḥuqúq on a certain property, and the income from that property is equal to his needs, no Ḥuqúq is payable by that person.

"Ḥuqúq is not payable on agricultural tools and equipment, and on animals used in ploughing the land, to the extent that these are necessary."

—*'Abdu'l-Bahá, Compilation on Ḥuqúqu'lláh, p.41*

"Regarding the Ḥuqúqu'lláh, ...this is applied to one's merchandise, property and income. After deducting the necessary expenses, whatever is left as profit, and is an addition to one's capital, such a sum is subject to Ḥuqúq. When one has paid Ḥuqúq once on a particular sum, that sum is no longer subject to Ḥuqúq, unless it should pass from one person to another. One's residence, and the household furnishings are exempted from Ḥuqúq... Ḥuqúqu'lláh is paid to the Centre of the Cause."

—*Shoghi Effendi, Compilation on Ḥuqúqu'lláh,.p.48*

Note : Readers are advised to read the compilation on Ḥuqúqu'lláh compiled by the Research Department of the Universal House of Justice for a detail study of this subject.

INDUSTRIAL SLAVERY

"You did a wonderful thing in this country in 1865 when you abolished chattel slavery, but you must do a much more wonderful thing now, you must abolish industrial slavery!"

—*'Abdu'l-Bahá, Star of the West, Vol. VII, p. 6*

INHERITANCE

(a) Inheritance falls into the following categories:
    (1) Children   1,080 out of 2,520 shares
    (2) Husband or wife   390 out of 2,520 shares
    (3) Father   330 out of 2,520 shares
    (4) Mother   270 out of 2,520 shares
    (5) Brother   210 out of 2,520 shares
    (6) Sister   150 out of 2,520 shares
    (7) Teacher[22]   90 out of 2,520 shares

(b) The share of the children, as allotted by the Báb is doubled by Bahá'u'lláh, and an equal portion correspondingly reduced from each of the remaining beneficiaries.

(c) (i) In cases where there is no issue, the share of the children reverts to the House of Justice to be expended on orphans and widows and for whatever will profit mankind.

    (ii) If the son of the deceased be dead and leave issue, these will inherit the share of their father. If the daughter of the deceased be dead and leave issue, her share will have to be divided into the seven categories specified in the Most Holy Book.

(d) Should one leave off-spring but either part or all of the other categories of inheritors be non-existent, two-thirds of their shares reverts to the off-spring and one-third to the House of Justice.

(e) Should none of the specified beneficiaries exist, two-thirds of the inheritance reverts to the nephews and nieces of the deceased. If these do not exist, the same share reverts to the aunts and uncles; lacking these, to their sons and daughters. In any case, the remaining third reverts to the House of Justice.

(f) Should one leave none of the aforementioned heirs, the entire inheritance reverts to the House of Justice.

(g) The residence and the personal clothing of the deceased father pass to the male not to the female off-spring.[23] If there be several residences, the principal and most important one passes to the male off-spring. The remaining residences will, together with the other possessions of the deceased have to be divided among the heirs. If there be no male off-spring, two-thirds of the principal residence and the personal clothing of the deceased father will revert to the female issue and one-third to the House of Justice. In the case of the deceased mother, all her used clothing is to be equally divided amongst her daughters. Her unworn clothing, jewels and property must be divided among her heirs, as well as her used clothing if she leaves no daughter.

(h) Should the children of the deceased be minors, their share should either be entrusted to a reliable person or to a company for purposes of investment, until they attain the age of maturity. A share of the interest accrued should be assigned to the trustee.

(i) The inheritance should not be divided until after the payment of the Ḥuqúqu'lláh[24] (The Right of God), of any debts contracted by the deceased and of any expenses incurred for a befitting funeral and burial.

(j) If the brother of the deceased is from the same father, he will inherit his full allotted share. If he is from another father, he will inherit only two-thirds of his share, the remaining one third reverting to the House of Justice. The same law is applicable to the sister of the deceased.

(k) In case there are full brothers or full sisters, brothers and sisters from the mother's side do not inherit.

(l) A non-Bahá'í teacher does not inherit. If there should be more than one teacher, the share allotted to the teacher is to be equally divided among them.

(m) Non-Bahá'í heirs do not inherit[25].

(n) Aside from the wife's used clothing and gifts of jewellery or otherwise which have been proven to have been given her by her husband, whatever the husband has purchased for his wife are to be considered as the husband's possessions to be divided among his heirs.

(o) Any person is at liberty to will his possessions as he sees fit provided he makes provisions for the payment of Ḥuqúqu'lláh and the discharge of his debts.

—*Synopsis and Codification of the Kitáb-i-Aqdas, p. 43*

"In future, a manufacturer will not be allowed to leave all his property to his own family. A law will be made something like this—that he must leave one-quarter only of his property to his family, and the other three-quarters must go to the factory workers who have created his wealth."

—*'Abdu'l-Bahá, Star of the West, Vol. VIII, p. 11.*

NOTES AND REFERENCES

22. When asked by an individual believer whether the term "teacher" referred to as one of the heirs meant a specific individual teacher or teachers, or whether the term could be applied generally, i.e. to education and learning the Guardian replied that the manner in which the law will be applied in this respect will be determined by the Universal House of Justice.

    —*Synopsis and Codification of the Kitáb-i-Aqdas, p. 43*

23. It has been explained by 'Abdu'l-Bahá that the residence and personal clothing of the deceased father go to the eldest son, or if he has predeceased his father, to the second son, and son on.

    —*Synopsis and Codification of the Kitáb-i-Aqdas, p. 40*

24. Huqúqu'lláh (The Right of God) : If a person has possessions equal in value to at least 19 mithqáls in gold, it is a spiritual obligation for him to pay 19% of the total amount, once only, a Huqúqu'lláh. Certain categories of possessions, such as one's residence, are exempt from this. Thereafter, whenever his income, after all expenses have been paid, increases the value of his possessions by the amount of at least 19 mithqáls of gold, he is to pay 19 of this increase, and so on for each further increase.

    —*Synopsis and Codification of the Kitáb-i-Aqdas, p. 45*

19. A mi<u>th</u>qál is a weight designated by the Báb,
     and is equivalent to a little over 3.5 grammes.

—*Synopsis and Codification of the Kitáb-i-Aqdas, pp. 40-42*

25. In a letter to the National Spiritual Assembly
     of the Bahá'ís of India, the Guardian's
     secretary wrote on his behalf: "Although in
     the *Questions and Answers,* Bahá'u'lláh has
     specifically stated that non-Bahá'ís have no
     right to inherit from their Bahá'í parents or
     relatives, yet this restriction applies only to
     such cases when a Bahá'í dies without
     leaving a will and when, therefore his
     property will have to be divided in
     accordance with the rules set forth in the
     Aqdas. Otherwise, a Bahá'í is free to bequeath
     his property to any person, irrespective of
     religion, provided however, he leaves a will,
     specifying his wishes. As you see therefore,
     it is always possible for a Bahá'í to provide
     for his non-Bahá'í wife, children or relatives
     by leaving a will, and it is only fair that he
     should do so."

—*Synopsis and Codification of the Kitáb-i-Aqdas, p. 45*

JUSTICE

"O SON OF SPIRIT !

The best beloved of all things in My sight is
Justice; turn not away therefrom if thou desirest Me,
and neglect it not that I may confide in thee. By its
aid thou shalt see with thine own eyes and not

through the eyes of others, and shalt know of thine own knowledge and not through the knowledge of thy neighbour. Ponder this in thy heart; how it behoveth thee to be. Verily justice is My gift to thee and the sign of My loving kindness. Set it then before thine eyes."

—*Bahá'u'lláh, The Hidden Words, from the Arabic. No. 2*

"They that are just and fair-minded in their judgement occupy a sublime station and hold an exalted rank. The light of piety and uprightness shineth resplendent from these souls. We earnestly hope that the peoples and countries of the world may not be deprived of the splendours of these two luminaries."

—*Bahá'u'lláh, The Third Ḥaráz, (Ornaments),*
Writings of Bahá'u'lláh, p. 188

"... The light of men is Justice. Quench it not with the contrary winds of oppression and tyranny. The purpose of Justice is the appearance of unity among men. The ocean of Divine wisdom surgeth within this exalted word, while the books of the world cannot contain its inner significance. Were mankind to be adorned with this raiment, they would behold the day-star of the utterance, 'On that day God will satisfy everyone out of His abundance,' (*cf. Qur'án 4:129*) shining resplendent above the horizon of the world. Appreciate ye the value of this utterance; it is a noble fruit that the Tree of the Pen of Glory hath yielded..."

—*Bahá'u'lláh, Sixth Leaf (Words of Paradise),*
Writings of Bahá'u'lláh, p. 20

"And among the Teachings of His Holiness, Bahá'u'lláh, are justice and right. Until these are

realized on the plane of existence, all things will be
in disorder and remain imperfect."

—*'Abdu'l-Bahá, Foundations of World Unity, p. 45*

"We ask God to endow human souls with justice
so that they may be fair, and may strive to provide
for the comfort of all, that each member of humanity
may pass his life in the utmost comfort and welfare.
Then this material world will become the very
paradise of the Kingdom, this elemental earth will
be in a heavenly state and all the servants of God
will live in the utmost joy, happiness and gladness."

—*'Abdu'l-Bahá, Star of the West, p. 230*

"In reality, so far great injustice has befallen the
common people."

—*'Abdu'l-Bahá, Star of the West, p. 231*

"The government of the countries should conform
to the Divine Law which gives equal justice to all.
This is the only way in which the deplorable
superfluity of great wealth and miserable,
demoralizing, degrading poverty can be abolished.
Not until this is done will the Law of God be
obeyed."

—*'Abdu'l-Bahá, Paris Talks, p. 154*

"Among the results of the Manifestation of
spiritual forces will be that the human world will
adapt itself to a new social form, the Justice of God
will become manifest throughout human affairs and
human equality will be universally established.

"The essence of the matter is that Divine Justice
will become manifest in human conditions and affairs

and all mankind will find comfort and enjoyment in life."

—'Abdu'l-Bahá, The Promulgation of Universal Peace, p. 132

MAN—NOT MERE FACTOR
IN PRODUCTION

"The station of man is great, were he to cling to truth and righteousness and be firm and steadfast in the Cause. Before the God of Mercy, a true man appears like unto heaven. The sun and the moon of that heaven are his sight and hearing and its stars are his shining attributes. His station is the highest and his signs are the educator of the world."

—Bahá'u'lláh, Kitáb-i-'Ahd, Bahá'í World Faith, p. 208

"... Man possesses conscious intelligence and reflection; nature is minus. This is an established fundamental among philosophers. Man is endowed with volition and memory; nature has neither. Man can seek out the mysteries latent in nature whereas nature is not conscious of her own hidden phenomena. Man is progressive; nature is stationary, without the power of progression or retrogression. Man is endowed with ideal virtues, for example intellection, volition,—among them faith, confession and acknowledgement of God, while nature is devoid of all these. The ideal faculties of man, including the capacity of scientific acquisition are beyond nature's ken. These are powers whereby man is differentiated and distinguished from all other forms of life..."

—'Abdu'l-Bahá, Foundations of World Unity, p. 61

MODERATION

"... In all matters moderation is desirable. If a thing is carried to excess, it will prove a source of evil. Consider the civilization of the West, how it hath agitated and alarmed the peoples of the world. An infernal engine hath been devised, and hath proved so cruel a weapon of destruction that its like none hath ever witnessed or heard."

—Bahá'u'lláh, Ninth Leaf, Words of Paradise,
Writings of Bahá'u'lláh, p. 204

"Fear ye God, and take heed not to outstrip the bounds of moderation, and be numbered among the extravagent."

—Bahá'u'lláh, Bahá'í World Faith, p. 40

PROFESSIONS AND CRAFTS

Work and Profession

"... Whatever the progress of the machinery may be, man will have always to toil in order to earn his living. Effort is an inseparable part of man's life. It may take different forms with the changing conditions of the world, but it will be always present as a necessary element in our earthly existence. Life is after all a struggle. Progress is attained through struggle, and without such a struggle life ceases to have a meaning; it becomes even extinct. The progress of machinery has not made effort unnecessary. It has given it a new form, a new outlet."

—*From a letter written on behalf of Shoghi Effendi to an individual believer, December 26, 1935, Lights of Guidance*

"It is enjoined upon every one of you to engage in some form of occupation, such as crafts, trades and the like. We have graciously exalted your engagement in such work to the rank of worship unto God, the True One. Ponder ye in your hearts the grace and the blessings of God and render thanks unto Him at eventide and at dawn. Waste not your time in idleness and sloth. Occupy yourselves with that which profiteth yourselves and others. Thus hath it been decreed in this Tablet from whose horizon the day-star of wisdom and utterance shineth resplendent.

"The most despised of men in the sight of God are those who sit idly and beg. Hold yet fast unto the cord of material means, placing your whole trust in God, the Provider of all means. When anyone occupieth himself in a craft or trade, such occupation itself is regarded in the estimation of God as an act of worship; and this naught but a token of His infinite and all pervasive bounty."

—*Bahá'u'lláh, The twelfth Glad-Tidings, Writings of Bahá'u'lláh, p. 184*

"With reference to Bahá'u'lláh's Command concerning the engagement of the believers in some sort of profession; the Teachings are most emphatic on this matter, particularly the statement in the 'Aqdas' to this effect which makes it quite clear that idle people who lack the desire to work can have no place in the new World Order. As a corollary of this principle, Bahá'u'lláh further states that mendicity should not only be discouraged but entirely wiped out from the face of society. It is the duty of those who are in charge of the organization of society to give every individual the opportunity of acquiring the necessary talent in some kind of profession, and also the means of utilizing such a talent, both for its own sake and for the sake of earning the means of his livelihood. Every individual, no matter how handicapped and limited he may be, is under the obligation of engaging in some work or profession, for work, specially when performed in the spirit of service, is according to Bahá'u'lláh a form of worship. It has not only a utilitarian purpose, but has a value in itself, because it draws us nearer to God, and enables us to better grasp His purpose for us in this world. It is obvious, therefore, that the inheritance of wealth cannot make anyone immune from daily work."

—From a letter written on behalf of Shoghi Effendi
to the National Spiritual Assembly of the United States and
Canada, March 22, 1937, Lights of Guidance

"O MY SERVANTS !

Ye are the trees of My garden; ye must give forth goodly and wonderous fruits, that ye yourselves and others may profit therefrom. Thus it is incumbent on everyone to engage in crafts and professions, for therein lies the secret of wealth. O men of understanding! For results depend upon means, and the grace of God shall be all sufficient unto you. Trees that yield no fruit have been and will ever be for the fire.

"O MY SERVANT !

The basest of men are they that yield no fruit on earth. Such men are verily counted as among the dead, nay, better are the dead in the sight of God than those idle and worthless souls.

"O MY SERVANT !

The best of men are they that earn a livelihood by their calling and spend upon themselves and upon their kindred for the Love of God, the Lord of all Worlds."

—*Bahá'u'lláh, The Hidden Words, from the Persian, Nos. 80-82*

"... Having attained the stage of fulfilment and reached his maturity, man standeth in need of wealth, and such wealth as he acquireth through crafts or professions is commendable and praiseworthy in the estimation of men of wisdom, and especially in the eyes of servants who dedicate themselves to the education of the world and to the edification of its peoples..."

—*Bahá'u'lláh, The First Taráz, Writings of Bahá'u'lláh, p. 187*

Arts and Crafts

"... The people of Bahá should not deny any soul the reward due to him, should treat craftsmen with deference, and, unlike the people aforetime, should not defile their tongues with abuse.

"In this Day the sun of craftsmanship shineth above the horizon of the occident and the river of arts is flowing out of the sea of that region. One must speak with fairness and appreciate such bounty..."

—*Bahá'u'lláh, The Fifth Taráz, Writings of Bahá'u'lláh, p. 189*

"The third Tajallí is concerning arts, crafts and sciences. Knowledge is as wings to man's life, and a ladder for his ascent. Its acquisition is incumbent upon everyone. The knowledge of such sciences, however, should be acquired as can profit the peoples of the earth, and not those which begin with words and end with words. Great indeed is the claim of scientists and craftsmen on the peoples of the world..."

—*Bahá'u'lláh, The third Tajallí, Writings of Bahá'u'lláh, p. 195*

PENSION

"... The workmen should receive wages which assure them an adequate support and when they cease work, becoming feeble or helpless, they should receive from the owner of the factory a sufficient pension."

—*'Abdu'l-Bahá, Some Answered Questions, p. 315*

POOR AND NEEDY

"You must show forth that which will be conducive to the welfare and tranquillity of the helpless ones of the world."

—*Bahá'u'lláh, Tablet of the World, Bahá'í World Faith, p. 173*

"Know ye that the poor are the trust of God in your midst. Watch that ye betray not His trust, that ye deal not unjustly with them and that ye walk not in the ways of the treacherous. Ye will most certainly be called upon to answer for His trust on the day when the Balance of Justice shall be set, the day when unto everyone shall be rendered his due, when the doings of all men, be they rich or poor, shall be weighed."

—*Bahá'u'lláh, Bahá'í World Faith, pp. 40-41*

"If a person is unable to earn his own living, it is incumbent upon the House of Justice and the wealthy to provide for him."

—*Synopsis and Codification of the Kitáb-i-Aqdas, p. 63*

"O SON OF MAN !

Should prosperity befall thee, rejoice not, and should abasement come upon thee, grieve not, for both shall pass away and be no more.

"O SON OF BEING !

If poverty overtake thee, be not sad; for in time the Lord of wealth shall visit thee. Fear not abasement, for glory shall one day rest on thee.

"O SON OF MAN !

Bestow My wealth upon My poor, that in heaven thou mayest draw from stores of unfading splendour and treasures of imperishable glory. But by My life! to offer up thy soul is a more glorious thing couldst thou but see with Mine eye."

—*Bahá'u'lláh, The Hidden Words, from the Arabic, Nos. 52, 53 and 57*

"O CHILDREN OF DUST !

Tell the rich of the midnight sighing of the poor, lest heedlessness lead them into the path of destruction, and deprive them of the Tree of wealth. To give and to be generous are attributes of Mine; well is it with him that adorneth himself with My virtues.

"O SON OF MY HANDMAID !

Be not troubled in poverty nor confident in riches, for poverty is followed by riches, and riches are followed by poverty. Yet to be poor in all save God is a wonderous gift, belittle not the value thereof, for in the end it will make thee rich in God, and thus, thou shalt know the meaning of the utterance, "In truth ye are the poor' and the holy words: "God is the all-possessing' shall even as the true morn break forth gloriously resplendent upon the horizon of the lover's heart, and abide secure on the throne of wealth.

"O YE RICH ONES ON EARTH !

The poor in your midst, are My trust; guard ye My trust, and be not intent only on your own ease."

— *Bahá'u'lláh, The Hidden Words, from the Persian, Nos. 49, 51 and 54*

"O people of wealth and riches! If you see a poor man suffering from any calamity, do not run away from him but sit with him and ask him about the things heaped upon him from the seas of determination and predestination."

— *'Abdu'l-Bahá, from the Tablet "To Guide the Guides", The Bahá'í World, Vol. IV, p. 453*

"Then the orphans will be looked after, all of whose expenses will be taken care of. The cripples in the village—all their expenses will be looked after. The poor in the village—their necessary expenses will be defrayed. And other members who for valid reasons are incapacitated—the blind, the old, the deaf—their comfort must be looked after. In the village, no one will remain in need or in want."

— *'Abdu'l-Bahá, Star of the West, Vol. XIII, p. 229*

"The rich will enjoy the privilege of this new economic condition, as well as the poor, for owing to certain provision and restriction they will not be able to accumulate so much as to be burdened by its management, while the poor will be relieved from the stress of want and misery. The rich will enjoy his palace and the poor will have his comfortable cottage."

—*'Abdu'l-Bahá, The Promulgation of Universal Peace, p. 132*

"What could be better before God than thinking of the poor. For the poor are beloved by our Heavenly Father. When Christ came upon the earth, those who believed in Him and followed Him, were the poor and lowly, showing that the poor were near to God..."

—*'Abdu'l-Bahá, The Promulgation of Universal Peace, p. 216*

"They who are possessed of riches, however, must have the utmost regard for the poor, for great in the honour destined by God for those poor who are steadfast in patience. By My life! There is no honour, except what God may please to bestow, that can compare to this honour. Great is the blessedness awaiting the poor that endure patiently and conceal their sufferings, and well is it with the rich who bestow their riches on the needy and prefer them before themselves.

"Please God, the poor may exert themselves and strive to earn the means of livelihood. This is a duty which, in this most great Revelation, hath been prescribed unto every one, and is accounted in the sight of God as a goodly deed. Whoso observeth this duty, the help of the invisible One shall most certainly aid him. He can enrich, through His grace, whomsoever He pleaseth. He, verily, hath power over all things..."

—*Bahá'u'lláh, Gleanings from the Writings of Bahá'u'lláh,*
pp. 202-203

"Regarding your question concerning helping the poor: The Bahá'ís should not go so far as to refrain from extending charity to the needy, if they are able and willing to do so. However, in this, as in many other things, they should exert moderation. The greatest gift that we can give to the poor and the down-trodden is to aid to build up the divine institutions inaugurated in this day by Bahá'u'lláh, as these institutions, and this World Order when established, will eliminate the causes of poverty and the injustices which afflict the poor. We should, therefore, do both support our Bahá'í Fund, and also be kind and generous to the needy."

—*From a letter written on behalf of Shoghi Effendi to*
an individual believer, March II, 1942

ROLE OF GOVERNMENTS
IN ECONOMIC AFFAIRS

"Under their advice a place must be appointed, and they must assemble together in that place, and hold fast to the rope of consultation, and decide upon and execute that which is conducive to the people's security, affluence, welfare and tranquillity."

—*Bahá'u'lláh, Bahá'í World Faith, Tablet of the Wrold, p. 178*

"It is incumbent upon the Trustees of the House of Justice to take counsel together regarding such laws as have not been expressly revealed in the Book. Of these whatever they deem advisable and proper that must they enforce."

—*Bahá'u'lláh, Bahá'í World Faith, Words of Paradise, p. 182*

"All the governments of the world must be united and organize an assembly the members of which should be elected from the parliaments and the nobles of the nations. These must plan with utmost wisdom and power so that neither the capitalists suffer from enormous losses nor the labourers become needy. In the utmost moderation they should make the law; then announce to the public that the rights of the working people are to be strongly preserved. Also the rights of the capitalists are to be protected. When such a general plan is adopted by the will of both sides, should a strike occur, all the governments of the world collectively should resist it. Otherwise, the labour problem will lead to much destruction."

—*'Abdu'l-Bahá, Star of the West, Vol. XIII, p. 231*

"The interference of Courts of Justice and of the Government in difficulties pending between manufacturers and workmen is legal, for the reason that current affairs between workmen and manufacturers cannot be compared with ordinary affairs between private persons, which do not concern the public, and with which the Government should not occupy itself. In reality, although they appear to be matters between private persons, these difficulties between patrons and workmen produce a general detriment; for commerce, industry, agriculture and the general affairs of the country are

all intimately linked together. If one of these suffers
an abuse, the detriment affects the mass. Thus the
difficulties between workmen and manufacturers
become a cause of general detriment.

"The Court of Justice and the Government have
therefore the right of interference..."

—*'Abdu'l-Bahá, Some Answered Questions, p. 317*

"A World Federal System, ruling the whole earth
and exercising unchallengeable authority over its
unimaginably vast resources, blending and
embodying the ideals of both the East and the West,
liberated from the curse of war and its miseries, and
bent on the exploitation of all the available sources
of energy on the surface of the planet, a system in
which Force is made the servant of Justice, whose
life is sustained by its universal recognition of one
God and by its allegiance to one common
Revelation—such is the goal towards which
humanity, impelled by the unifying forces of life, is
moving."

—*Shoghi Effendi, The World Order of Bahá'u'lláh, p. 204*

"This commonwealth must, as far as we can
visualize it, consist of a World Legislature, whose
members will, as the trustees of the whole of
mankind, ultimately control the entire resources of all
the component nations, and will enact such laws as
shall be required to regulate the life, satisfy the
needs and adjust the relationships of all races and
peoples. A world executive, backed by an
international Force, will carry out the decisions
arrived at, and apply the laws enacted by, this world

legislature, and will safeguard the organic unity of the whole commonwealth. A World Tribunal will adjudicate and deliver its compulsory and final verdict in all and any disputes that may arise between the various elements constituting this universal system. A mechanism of world inter-communication' will be devised, embracing the whole planet freed from national hindrances and restrictions, and functioning with marvellous swiftness and perfect regularity. A world metropolis will act as the nerve center of a world civilization, the focus towards which the unifying forces of life will converge and from which its energizing influences will radiate."

—*Shoghi Effendi, The World Order of Bahá'u'lláh, p. 203*

REPRESENTATIVES OF THE WAGE-EARNING CLASSES

"... In the industrial world, where the representatives of the wage-earning classes, either through violence or persuasion, are capturing the seats of authority and wielding the scepter of power.... In the heart of society itself, where the ominous signs of increasing extravagance and profligacy are but lending fresh impetus to the forces of revolt and reaction that are growing more distinct every day—in these as in many others we have much cause for alarm, but much to be hopeful and thankful also."

—*Shoghi Effendi, Bahá'í Administration, p. 146*

RATE OF INTEREST

"... Most of the people are found to be in need
of this matter, for if no interest be allowed, affairs
(business) will be tramelled and obstructed... A
person is rarely found who would lend money to
anyone upon the principle of 'Qarḍ-i-ḥasan' (literally
'good loan', i.e. money advanced without interest
and repaid at the pleasure of the borrower).
Consequently, out of favour to the servants, We have
appointed 'profit on money' to be current, among
other business transactions which are in force among
people. That is ... it is allowable, lawful and pure to
charge interest on money... but this matter must be
conducted with moderation and justice. The Pen of
Glory has withheld itself from laying down its limits,
as a Wisdom from his Presence and as a
convenience for His servants. We exhort the friends
of God to act with fairness and justice, and in such
a way that the mercy of His beloved ones, and their
compassion, may be manifested towards each other...
"The execution of these matters has been placed
in charge of the men of the House of Justice, in order
that they may act in accordance with the exigencies
of the time and with wisdom."

—*Bahá'u'lláh, Tablet of Ishráqát, Bahá'u'lláh
and the New Era, pp. 136-137*

RETIREMENT

"As to the question of retirement from work for
individuals who have reached a certain age, this is

a matter on which the International House of Justice will have to legislate as there are no provisions in the Aqdas concerning it."

—*Shoghi Effendi, Principles of Bahá'í Administration, p. 12*

"Even though you are 79 years old, that does not seem in your case to be any handicap; and in this Cause, as the Guardian has told us there is work for everyone of some sort, of whatever age he or she may be."

—*Written on behalf of the Guardian to an individual believer August 23, 1954; cited by the Universal House of Justice, December 14, 1970, Lights of Guidance*

STRIKES

"You have questioned me about strikes. This question is and will be for a long time the subject of great difficulties. Strikes are due to two causes. One is the extreme sharpness and rapacity of the capitalists and manufacturers; the other the excesses, the avidity and ill-will of the workmen and artisans. It is therefore necessary to remedy these two causes.

"But the principal cause of these difficulties lies in the laws of the present civilization; for they lead to a small number of individuals accumulating incomparable fortunes, beyond their needs, whilst the greater number remains destitute, stripped and in the greatest misery. This is contrary to justice, to humanity, to equity; it is the height of inequity, the opposite to what causes divine satisfaction.

"This contrast is peculiar to the world of man: with other creatures, that is to say with nearly all

animals, there is a kind of justice and equality. Thus
in a shepherd's flock of sheep, in a troop of deer in
the country, among the birds of the prairie, of the
plain, of the hill or of the orchard, almost every
animal receives a just share based on equality. With
them such a difference in the means of existence is
not to be found: so they live in the most complete
peace and joy.

"It is quite otherwise with the human species,
which persists in the greatest error, and in absolute
iniquity. Consider an individual who has amassed
treasures by colonising a country for his profit: he
has obtained an incomparable fortune, and has
secured profits and incomes which flow like a river,
whilst a hundred thousand unfortunate people, weak
and powerless, are in need of a mouthful of bread.
There is neither equality nor brotherhood. So you see
that general peace and joy are destroyed, the welfare
of humanity is partially annihilated, and that
collective life is fruitless. Indeed, fortune, honours,
commerce, industry are in the hands of some
industrials, whilst other people are submitted to
quite a series of difficulties and to limitless troubles:
they have neither advantages nor profits, nor
comforts, nor peace.

"Then rules and laws should be established to
regulate the excessive fortunes of certain private
individuals, and limit the misery of millions of the
poor masses; thus a certain moderation would be
obtained. However, absolute equality is just as
impossible, for absolute equality in fortunes, honours,
commerce, agriculture, industry would end in a want
of comfort, in discouragement, in disorganisation of
the means of existence, and in universal

disappointment: the order of the community would be quite destroyed. Thus, there is a great wisdom in the fact that equality is not imposed by law: it is, therefore, preferable for moderation to do its work. The main point is, by means of laws and regulations to hinder the constitution of the excessive fortunes of certain individuals, and to protect the essential needs of the masses. For instance, the manufacturers and the industrials heap up a treasure each day, and the poor artisans do not gain their daily sustenance; that is the height of iniquity, and no just man can accept it. Therefore, laws and regulations should be established which would permit the workmen to receive from the factory owner their wages and a share in the fourth or the fifth part of the profits, according to the wants of the factory; or in some other way the body of workmen and the manufacturers should share equitably the profits and advantages. Indeed, the direction and administration of affairs come from the owner of the factory, and the work and labour, from the body of the workmen. In other words, the workmen should receive wages which assure them an adequate support, and when they cease work, becoming feeble or helpless, they should receive from the owner of the factory a sufficient pension. The wages should be high enough to satisfy the workmen with the amount they receive, so that they may be able to put a little aside for days of want and helplessness.

"When matters will be thus fixed, the owner of the factory will no longer put aside daily a treasure which he has absolutely no need of, (without taking into consideration that if the fortune is disproportionate, the capitalist succumbs under a formidable burden, and gets into the greatest difficulties and troubles; the administration of an excessive fortune is very difficult, and exhausts man's natural strength). And, the workmen and artisans will no longer be in the greatest misery and want, they will no longer be submitted to the worst privations at the end of their life.

"It is, then, clear and evident that the repartition of excessive fortunes amongst a small number of individuals, while the masses are in misery is an iniquity and an injustice. In the same way, absolute equality would be an obstacle to life, to welfare, to order and to the peace of humanity. In such a question a just medium is preferable. It lies in the capitalists being moderate in the acquisition of their profits, and in their having a consideration for the welfare of the poor and needy; that is to say, that the workmen and artisans receive a fixed and established daily wage, and have a share in the general profits of the factory.

"It would be well, with regard to the social rights of manufacturers, workmen and artisans, that laws be established, giving moderate profits to manufacturers, and to workmen the necessary means of existence and security for the future. Thus, when they become feeble and cease working, get old and helpless, and die leaving children under age, these children will not be annihilated by excess of poverty. And it is from the income of the factory itself, to which they have a right, that they will derive a little of the means of existence.

"In the same way, the workmen should no longer rebel and revolt, nor demand beyond their rights; they should no longer go out on strike, they should be obedient and submissive, and not ask for impudent wages. But the mutual rights of both associated parties will be fixed and established according to custom by just and impartial laws. In case one of the two parties should transgress, the courts of justice would have to give judgement, and by an efficacious fine put an end to the transgression; thus order will be re-established, and the difficulties settled. The interference of courts of justice and of the Government in difficulties pending between manufacturers and workmen is legal, for the reason that current affairs between workmen and manufacturers cannot be compared with ordinary affairs between private persons, which do not concern the public, and with which the Government should not occupy itself. In reality, although they appear to be matters between private persons, these difficulties between patrons and workmen produce a general detriment; for commerce, industry, agriculture and the general affairs of the country are all intimately linked together. If one of these suffers an abuse, the detriment affects the mass. Thus the difficulties between workmen and manufacturers become a cause of general detriment.

"The court of justice and the Government have therefore the right of interference. When a difficulty occurs between two individuals with reference to private rights, it is necessary for a third to settle the question: this is the part of the Government: then the question of strikes—which cause troubles in the country and are often connected with the excessive vexations of the workmen, as well as with the rapacity of manufacturers how could it remain neglected?

"Good God! is it possible that, seeing one of his

fellow creatures starving, destitute of everything, a man can rest and live comfortably in his luxurious mansion? He who meets another in the greatest misery, can he enjoy his fortune? That is why, in the Religion of God, it is prescribed and established that wealthy men each year give over a certain part of their fortune for the maintenance of the poor and unfortunate. That is the foundation of the Religion of God, and the most essential of the Commandments.

"As now man is not forced nor obliged by the Government, if by the natural tendency of his good heart, with the greatest spirituality, he goes to this expense for the poor, this will be a thing very much praised, approved and pleasing.

"Such is the meaning of the good works in the Divine Books and Tablets..."

—*'Abdu'l-Bahá, Some Answered Questions, pp. 313-316*

"Today the method of demand is the strike and resort to force which is manifestly wrong and destructive of human foundations. Rightful privilege and demand must be set forth in laws and regulations."

—*'Abdu'l-Bahá, Promulgation of Universal Peace, p. 238*

SOCIALIZATION

"The question of socialization is very important. It will not be solved by strikes for wages."

—*'Abdu'l-Bahá, Star of the West, Vol. XIII, p. 231*

SCIENCE AND TECHNOLOGY

"Science cannot create unity and fellowship in human hearts."

—*'Abdu'l-Bahá, Star of the West, Vol. XIII, p. 232*

"The development and progress of a nation is according to the measure and degree of that nation's scientific attainments. Through this means, its greatness is continually increased and day by day the welfare and prosperity of its people are assured."

—*'Abdu'l-Bahá, Foundations of World Unity, p. 60*

"A Scientific man is a true index and representative of humanity, for through processes of inductive reasoning and research he is informed of all that appertains to humanity, its status, conditions and happenings. He studies the human body politic, understands social problems and weaves the web and texture of civilization. In fact, science may be likened to a mirror wherein the infinite forms and images of existing things are revealed and reflected. It is the very foundation of all individual and national development. Without this basis of investigation, development is impossible."

—*'Abdu'l-Bahá, Foundations of World Unity, p. 61*

STOREHOUSE AND TAXATION

Storehouse (Village)

"The solution begins with the village, and when the village is reconstructed, then the cities will be also. The idea is this, that in each village will be erected a storehouse. In the language of Religion it is called the House of Finance. That is a universal storehouse which is commenced in the village. Its administration is through a committee of the wise ones of the community, and with the approval of that committee all the affairs are directed."

—*'Abdu'l-Bahá, Light of the World, p. 45.*
The Bahá'í World, Vol. IV, p. 450

"In brief, from among the wise men in every village, a board should be organized and the affairs of that village be under the control of that board. Likewise a general storehouse should be founded with the appointment of a secretary. At the time of the harvest, with the approval of the members of that board—a determined percent of the entire harvest be appropriated for the storehouse."

—*Extract from a Tablet of 'Abdu'l-Bahá, dated October 4, 1912, to an individual believer, sent by the Universal House of Justice to the compiler*

"The board of the house of finance (storehouse) will direct in every village the revenues of the house such as tithes, tax on animals, etc. In every village a storehouse and an officer-in-charge are to be provided while the notables of the village gather and form a board and to this board and officer the direction of the affairs of the village are entrusted. They take charge of all the questions pertaining to the village and the revenues of the storehouse such as tithes, tax on animals and other revenues are gathered in it and are given out for necessary expenditures."

—*Extract from a Tablet of 'Abdu'l-Bahá, dated July 25, 1919, to an individual believer, sent by the Universal House of Justice to the compiler*

Storehouse (City)

"For larger cities, naturally, there will be a system on a larger scale. Were I to go into that solution the details thereof would be very lengthy."

—'Abdu'l-Bahá, Star of the West, Vol. XIII, p. 229

Great House of Justice

"If there is something left over (after these expenditures), it should be given to the Great House of Justice. And thus there will be no want in the village. The people will not remain hungry, they will not remain naked. All will be in the utmost welfare and comfort."

—'Abdu'l-Bahá, The Bahá'í World, Vol. IV, p. 451

Storehouse (Revenues)

"This store house is to have seven revenues: Tithes, taxes on animals, wealth without inheritors, all things found whose owners cannot be discovered, a third of all treasures (money) found in the earth, a third of the mines—and voluntary contributions."

—Extract from a Tablet of 'Abdu'l-Bahá, dated October 4, 1912, to an individual believer, sent by the Universal House of the Justice to the compiler

"As to the revenues of the storehouse, the House of Justice must strive by every means possible to increase that amount, i.e. by every just means."

—Extract from a Tablet of 'Abdu'l-Bahá, dated July 25, 1919, to an individual believer, sent by the Universal House of Justice to the compiler

"First, whatever contributions are necessary, they obtain from the bank at interest. For instance, they borrow from the bank at three percent and loan to the public at four percent. Any farmer who is in need of implements, they supply and give him all his necessities. When the crop is harvested, it will be the first income of the storehouse. The first revenue is this. But this revenue is not equally distributed. For instance, a person may have a crop of one thousand kilos and this is only sufficient for his wants and living. From him nothing will be taken because he needs it all. If something is taken from him, he will remain hungry.

"But again, there may be one whose needs require one thousand kilos and his income is two thousand kilos. From him one-tenth is taken. Again, one needs two thousand kilos, but his income is ten thousand kilos. From him two-tenths will be taken. He needs two thousand kilos. If two thousand are taken from him he still has six thousand remaining.

"One has fifty thousand kilos, from him one-third is taken. One may have ten thousand kilos expenses, but has one hundred thousand kilos income. One half is taken. The greater the income, the greater is the ratio of taxation.

"Second: It is also the same with the cattle. They take proportionately the revenue from the cattle. For example, if a man has two cows necessary for his wants, nothing is taken from him. The more he has, the more is taken from him. This is the second revenue.

"The third revenue of the storehouse comes from one who dies without heirs.

"The fourth revenue comes from mines. If a mine is found upon the land of a person, one-third of it belongs to him and the remainder to the storehouse.

"The fifth revenue is hidden treasure. If a person finds a hidden treasure in the earth, he takes half of it, and the other half goes to the storehouse.

"The sixth revenue. If it (treasure) is found on the way, also half of it belongs to the storehouse.

"The seventh revenue is voluntary contributions to the storehouse. Of their own free will and with utmost willingness, the people will give."

—*'Abdu'l-Bahá, Light of the World, p. 45.*
The Bahá'í World, Vol. IV. p. 450

Storehouse (Expenditure)

"On the other hand there are seven expenditures:

1. General running expenses of the Institution—salaries etc; and the administration of public safety; including hygienic department.
2. Tithes—to the General Government (State).
3. Taxes on animals for the State.
4. Support of orphanage.
5. Support of cripples and incurables.
6. Support of educational institutions.
7. Supplying any deficiency in the expenses of the poor."

—*Extract from a Tablet of 'Abdu'l-Bahá, dated October 4, 1912,*
to an individual believer, sent by the Universal
House of Justice to the compiler.

"Likewise with the expenditures; if anything is deemed necessary for the village such as providing of hygienic measures, the House of Justice must also make all the necessary provision. In short, if it is done in this manner in the village, the orphans, the disabled and the poor will secure the means of subsistence; education will be fostered, and the adoption of hygienic measures will become universal.

"These are only the preliminary principles, the

House of Justice will arrange and widen them in accordance with time and place."

—*Extract from a Tablet of 'Abdu'l-Bahá, dated July 25, 1919, to an individual believer, sent by the Universal House of Justice to the compiler.*

"These are the seven revenues, but there are seven fixed expenditures.

"The first expenditure: The storehouse ought to give one-tenth to the Government, to the public treasury for the public expenses.

"The second expenditure is for the poor. The poor who are in need, those who are exempt, not those who are idle. For instance, if a person's crop is burned or he has a loss in his business, and for this reason has become poor, these poor people are to be taken care of.

"Third, the infirm, who come to want and cannot work.

"Fourth, the orphans. To them also help must be given.

"Fifth, the schools. The schools must be organized for the education of the children.

"Sixth, for the deaf and blind.

"Seventh, public health. Whatever is necessary for the public health must be arranged. Swamps should be filled in, water should be brought in; whatever is necessary for the public health."

—*'Abdu'l-Bahá, Light of the World, The Bahá'í World,* Vol. IV, p. 451

National Treasury

"... if after all these expenses are defrayed, any surplus is found in the storehouse, it must be transferred to the National Treasury."

—*'Abdu'l-Bahá, Star of the West, December 1922, Vol. XIII, p. 229*

"If anything is left in the storehouse, that must be transferred to the general treasury of the nation for general national expenses."

—*Letter of 'Abdu'l-Bahá dated October 4, 1912, to an individual,
sent by the Universal House of Justice to the compiler.*

Trustees

"Certain trustees will be elected by the people in a given village to look after these transactions."

—*'Abdu'l-Bahá, Star of the West, December 1922, Vol. XIII, p. 229*

Trusts

"No more trusts will remain in the future. The question of the trusts will be wiped away entirely."

—*'Abdu'l-Bahá, Star of the West, Vol. XIII, p. 231*

Taxation

"We see you adding every year unto your expenditures and laying the burden thereof on the people whom ye rule; this verily is naught but grievous injustice. Fear the sighs and tears of this Wronged One, and burden not your peoples beyond that which they can endure."

—*Bahá'u'lláh, Tablet to Queen Victoria,
The World Order of Bahá'u'lláh, p. 40*

"We will find out, for instance, what is his annual revenue and also what are his expenditures. Now, if his income be equal to his expenditures, from such a farmer nothing whatever will be taken. That is, he will not be subjected to taxation of any sort, needing as he does all his income. Another farmer may have expenses running up to one thousand dollars, we will say, and his income is two thousand dollars. From such a-one, a-tenth will be required, because he has a surplus. But if his income be ten thousand dollars and his expenses one thousand dollars, or his income twenty thousand dollars he will have to pay on taxes one fourth. If his income be one hundred thousand dollars and his expenses five thousand, one-third will he have to pay because he has still a surplus, since his expenses are five thousand and his income one hundred thousand. If he pays, say, thirty-five thousand dollars, in addition to the expenditure of five thousand, he still has sixty thousand left. But if his expenses be ten thousand and his income two hundred thousand, then he must give an even half, because ninety thousand will be in that case, the sum remaining. Such as scale as this will determine allotment of taxes. All the income from such revenues will go to this general storehouse."

— *'Abdu'l-Bahá, Star of thw West, Vol. XIII, pp. 228-229*

"Each person in the community whose need is equal to his individual producing capacity shall be exempt from taxation. But if the income is greater than his needs he must pay, a man's capacity for production and his needs will be equalized and reconciled through taxation. If his production exceeds, he will pay a tax; if his necessities exceed his production he shall receive an amount sufficient to equalize or adjust. Therefore taxation will be proportionate to capacity and production and there will be no poor in the community.

"Bahá'u'lláh likewise commanded the rich to give freely to the poor. In the Kitáb-i-Aqdas it is further written by Him that those who have a certain amount of income must give one-fifth of it to God the Creator of heaven and earth."

—*'Abdu'l-Bahá, The Promulgation of Universal Peace, p. 217*

TARIFFS AND OTHER ECONOMIC BARRIERS

"That a narrow and brutal nationalism, which the postwar theory of self-determination has served to reinforce, has been chiefly responsible for the policy of high and prohibitive tariffs, so injurious to the healthy flow of international trade and to the mechanism of international finance, is a fact which few would venture to dispute."

—*Shoghi Effendi, The World Order of Bahá'u'lláh, p. 35*

"A world community in which all economic barriers will have been permanently demolished and the inter-dependence of Capital and Labour definitely recognized."

—*Shoghi Effendi, quoted in The Renewal of Civilization, p. 92*

TRADE UNIONS

"Regarding your questions about trade unions: The Guardian considers that this is a matter for each National Spiritual Assembly to advise the believers on. As long as the trade unions are not members of any particular political party, there does not seem to be any objection to the Bahá'ís belonging to them."

—*From the Guardian's secretary on his behalf in a letter
dated 2 February 1951, Lights of Guidance*

TITHES

"In respect to tithes Bahá'u'lláh has ordained that what is prescribed in the Qur'án should be followed. In general the law imposes an obligation to give a portion of one's assets for the relief of the poor for various other charitable purposes and to aid the Faith of God. The details of the application of this law are left to the Universal House of Justice to decide in future and the Guardian has stated that in the meantime the believers may contribute regularly and according to their means to the Bahá'í Fund."

—*Synopsis and Codification of the Kitáb-i-Aqdas, p. 63*

UNEMPLOYMENT

"That inter-governmental debts have imposed a severe strain on the masses of the people in Europe, have upset the equilibrium of national budgets, have crippled national industries, and led to an increase in the number of the unemployed, is no less apparent to an unprejudiced observer."

—*Shoghi Effendi, The World Order of Bahá'u'lláh, p. 35*

USE OF TECHNICAL KNOW-HOW

"According to some accounts, mankind has been directed to borrow various good qualities and ways from wild animals and to learn a lesson from these. Since it is permissible to imitate virtues of dumb animals, it is certainly far more so to borrow material sciences and techniques from foreign peoples, who atleast belong to the human race and are distinguished by judgement and the power of speech. And if it be contended that such praiseworthy qualities are inborn in animals, by what proof can they claim that these essential principles of civilization, this knowledge and these sciences current among other peoples, are not inborn?"

—*'Abdu'l-Bahá, The Secret of Divine Civilization, p. 30*

"It has now been clearly and irrefutably shown that the importation from foreign countries of the principles and procedures of civilization, and the acquisition from them of sciences and techniques, in brief, of whatsoever will contribute to the general good, is entirely permissible."

—*'Abdu'l-Bahá, The Secret of Divine Civilization, p. 31*

"Can we maintain that it is contrary to the fundamentals of the Faith to encourage the acquisition of useful arts and of general knowledge, to inform oneself as to the truths of such physical sciences as are beneficial to man, and to widen the scope of industry and increase the products of commerce and multiply the nation's avenues of wealth? Would it conflict with the worship of God to establish law and order in the cities and organize the rural districts, to repair the roads and build railroads and facilitate transportation and travel and thus increase the people's well-being? Would it be inconsistent with the Divine commands and prohibitions if we were to work the abandoned mines which are the greatest source of the nation's wealth, and to build factories, from which come the entire people's comfort, security and affluence? Or to stimulate the creation of new industries and to promote improvement in our domestic products?

—'Abdu'l-Bahá, *The Secret of Divine Civilization, pp. 101-102*

"One should regard the other technological advances, sciences, arts and political formulae of proven usefulness in the same light—i.e., those procedures which, down the ages, have time and again been put to the test and whose many uses and advantages have demonstrably resulted in the glory and greatness of the state, and the well-being and progress of the people. Should all these be abandoned, for no valid reason, and other methods of reform be attempted, by the time such reforms might eventuate, and their advantages might be put to proof, many years would go by, and many lives."

—'Abdu'l-Bahá, *The Secret of Divine Civilization, pp. 113-114*

WEALTH

"Wealth is praiseworthy in the highest degree, if it is acquired by an individual's own effort and the grace of God, in commerce, agriculture, art and industry, and if it be expended for philanthropic purposes. Above all, if a judicious and resourceful individual should initiate measures which would universally enrich the masses of the people, there could be no undertaking greater than this, and it would rank in the sight of God as the supreme achievement, for such a benefactor would supply the needs and insure the comfort and well-being of a great multitude. Wealth is most commendable, provided the entire population is wealthy. If, however, a few have inordinate riches while the rest are impoverished, and no fruit or benefit accrues from that wealth, then it is only a liability to its possessor. If, on the other hand, it is expended for the promotion of knowledge, the founding of elementary and other schools, the encouragement of art and industry, the training of orphans and the poor—in brief, if it is dedicated to the welfare of society—its possessors will stand out before God and man as the most excellent of all who live on earth and will be accounted as one of the people of paradise."

—*'Abdu'l-Bahá, The Secret of Divine Civilization, pp. 24-25*

Distribution of Wealth

"That the financial obligations contracted in the course of the war, as well as the imposition of a staggering burden of reparations upon the vanquished have, to a very great extent, been responsible for the maldistribution and consequent shortage of the world's monetary gold supply, which in turn has, to a very great measure, accentuated the phenomenal fall in prices and thereby relentlessly increased the burdens of impoverished countries, no impartial mind would question."

—*Shoghi Effendi, The World Order of Bahá'u'lláh, p. 35*

Limitation of Wealth

"Hearts must be so cemented together, love must become so dominant that the rich shall most willingly extend assistance to the poor and take steps to establish these economic adjustments permanently. If it is accomplished in this way it will be most praiseworthy because then it will be for the sake of God and in the pathway of His service."

—*Excerpts from a discourse made on July 23, 1912, in Boston by* '*Abdu'l-Bahá, World Order Magazine, Vol. XI, No. 12, March 1946*

"There must be special laws made, dealing with these extremes of riches and of want. The members of the Government should consider the laws of God when they are framing plans for the ruling of the people. The general rights of mankind must be guarded and preserved."

—'*Abdu'l-Bahá, Paris Talks, pp. 153-154*

"The rich too must be merciful to the poor, contributing from willing hearts to their needs without being forced or compelled to do so."

—'*Abdu'l-Bahá, The Promulgation of Universal Peace, p. 107*

"The greatest means for prevention is that whereby the laws of the community will be so framed and enacted that it will not be possible for a few to be millionaries and many destitute. One of Bahá'u'lláh's Teachings is the adjustment of means of livelihood in human society. Under this adjustment there can be no extremes in human conditions as regards wealth and sustenance."

—'*Abdu'l-Bahá, The Promulgation of Universal Peace, p. 216*

"Social inequality is the inevitable outcome of the

natural inequality of man. Human beings are different in ability and should, therefore, be different in their social and economic standing. Extremes of wealth and poverty should, however be abolished."

—*Shoghi Effendi, Directives from the Guardian, p. 20*

WORLD CURRENCY

"... a uniform and universal system of currency, of weights and measures, will simplify and facilitate intercourse and understanding among the nations and races of mankind..."

—*Shoghi Effendi, The Bahá'í Peace Program, p. 8*

WORKMAN AND INDUSTRY

Factory—Labourers and Workmen

"Laws must be made because it is impossible for the labourers to be satisfied with the present system. They will strike every month and every year. Finally, the capitalists will lose."

—*'Abdu'l-Bahá, Star of the West, Vol. XIII, p. 231*

"Indeed, the direction and administration of affairs come from the owner of the factory, and the work and labour, from the body of the workmen.

"In the same way, the workmen should no longer rebel and revolt, nor demand beyond their rights; they should no longer go out on strike, they should be obedient and submissive, and not ask for impudent wages. But the mutual rights of both associated parties will be fixed and established according to custom by just and impartial laws."

—*'Abdu'l-Bahá, Some Answered Questions, pp. 315-316*

Factory—Shares and Profit

"Therefore, laws and regulations should be established which would permit the workmen to receive from the factory owner their wages and a share in the fourth or the fifth part of the profits, according to the wants of the factory; or in some other way the body of workmen and the manufacturers should share equitably the profits and advantages.

"That is to say, that the workmen and artisans receive a fixed and established daily wage, and have a share in the general profits of the factory."

—*'Abdu'l-Bahá, Some Answered Questions, p. 315*

"Also, every factory that has ten thousand shares will give two thousand shares of these ten thousand to its employees and will write the shares in their names, so that they may have them, and the rest will belong to the capitalists. Then at the end of the month or year, whatever they may earn after the expenses and wages are paid, according to the number of shares, should be divided among both."

—*'Abdu'l-Bahá, Star of the West, Vol. XIII, p. 231*

WAGES

"The wages should be high enough to satisfy the

workmen with the amount they receive, so that they
may be able to put a little aside for days of want
and helplessness."

—'Abdu'l-Bahá, Some Answered Questions, p. 315

"Now I want to tell you about the law of God.
According to the Divine law, employees should not
be paid merely by wages. Nay, rather they should
be partners in every work."

—'Abdu'l-Bahá, Bahá'í Scriptures, p. 669, The Bahá'í World,
Vol. IV, p. 454

"The Master, has definitely stated that wages
should be unequal, simply because men are unequal
in their ability and hence should receive wages that
would correspond to their varying capacities and
resources."

—Shoghi Effendi, Directives from the Guardian, p. 20

"... The Master has definitely stated that wages
should be unequal, simply because that men are
unequal in their ability, and hence should receive
wages that would correspond to their varying
capacities and resources. This view seems to
contradict the opinion of some modern economists.
But the friends should have full confidence in the
words of the Master, and should give preference to
His statements over those voiced by our so-called
modern thinkers."

—From a letter written on behalf of Shoghi Effendi to an individual
believer, December 26, 1935, Lights of Guidance

WASTAGE ON WARS

"Peace is the pretext, and night and day they are all straining every nerve to pile up more weapons of war, and to pay for this their wretched people must sacrifice most of whatever they are able to earn by their sweat and toil. How many thousands have given up their work in useful industries and are labouring day and night to produce new and deadlier weapons which would spill out the blood of the race more copiously than before. Each day they invent a new bomb or explosive and then the governments must abandon their obsolete arms and begin producing the new, since the old weapons cannot hold their own against the new..."

—'*Abdu'l-Bahá, The Secret of Divine Civilization, p. 61*

"Observe that if such a happy situation be forthcoming, no government would need continually to pile up the weapons of war, nor feel itself obliged to produce ever new military weapons with which to conquer the human race. A small force for the purposes of internal security, the correction of criminal and disorderly elements and the prevention of local disturbances, would be required—no more. In this way the entire population would, first of all, be relieved of the crushing burden of expenditure currently imposed for military purposes, and secondly, great numbers of people would cease to devote their time to the continual devising of new weapons of destruction."

—'*Abdu'l-Bahá, The Secret of Divine Civilization, p. 65*

"The ministers of the House of Justice must promote the Most Great Peace, in order that the world may be freed from onerous expenditures. This matter is obligatory and indispensable; for warfare and conflict are the foundation of trouble and distress."

—*Bahá'u'lláh, Tablet of the World, Bahá'í World Faith, p. 176*

"... fathers, mothers, children in grief and lamentation, the foundations of life overturned, cities laid waste and fertile lands made desolate by the ravages of war."

—*'Abdu'l-Bahá, Foundations of World Unity, p. 10*

"If two nations were at war in olden times, ten or twenty thousand would be sacrificed but in this century the destruction of one hundred thousand lives in a day is quite possible. So perfected has the science of killing become and so efficient the means and instruments of its accomplishment, that a whole nation can be obliterated in a short time."

—*'Abdu'l-Bahá, Foundations of World Unity. p. 20*

"... the vast and ever-swelling army of the unemployed with its crushing burden and demoralizing influence on governments and people; the wicked, unbridled race of armaments swallowing an ever-increasing share of the substance of already impoverished nations."

—*Shoghi Effendi, World Order of Bahá'u'lláh, p. 32*

"... An enormous increase of national competitive armaments, involving during the last year the aggregate expenditure of no less than a thousand million pounds, which in turn has accentuated the effects of the world-wide depression, is a truth that even the most superficial observer will readily admit."

—*Shoghi Effendi, World Order of Bahá'u'lláh, p. 35*

"The enormous energy dissipated and wasted on war, whether economic or political will be consecrated to such ends as will extend the range of human inventions and technical development, to the increase of the productivity of mankind, to the extermination of disease, to the extension of scientific research, to the raising of the standard of physical health, to the sharpening and refinement of the human brain, to the exploitation of the unused and unsuspected resources of the planet, to the prolongation of human life, and to the furtherance of any other agency that can stimulate the intellectual, the moral, and spiritual life of the entire human race."

—*Shoghi Effendi, The Unfoldment of World Civilization,*
The World Order of Bahá'u'lláh, p. 204

WELFARE

"Each member of the body politic should live in the utmost comfort and welfare because each individual member of humanity is a member of the body politic and if one member of the members be in distress or be afflicted with some disease, all the other members must necessarily suffer."

—*'Abdu'l-Bahá, Star of the West, Vol. XIII, p. 227*

"The good pleasure of God consists in the welfare of all the individual members of mankind."

—*'Abdu'l-Bahá, Star of the West, Vol. XIII, p. 229*

"Bahá'u'lláh set forth principles of guidance and teaching for economic re-adjustment. Regulations were revealed by Him which insure the welfare of the commonwealth."

—'Abdu'l-Bahá, *The Promulgation of Universal Peace, p. 181*

"Human brotherhood and dependence exist because mutual helpfulness and co-operation are the two necessary principles underlying human welfare..."

—'Abdu'l-Bahá, *Foundations of World Unity, p. 14*

WORLD'S EQUILIBRIUM

"The world's equilibrium hath been upset through the vibrating influence of this most great, this New World Order. Mankind's ordered life hath been revolutionized through the agency of this unique, this wonderous system—the like of which mortal eyes have never witnessed."

—Bahá'u'lláh, *Synopsis and Codification of the Kitáb-i-Aqdas, p. 27*

"Say: This is the infallible Balance which the Hand of God is holding, in which all who are in the heavens and all who are on the earth are weighed, and their fate determined, if ye be of them that believe and recognize this truth."

—Bahá'u'lláh, *Synopsis and Codification of the Kitáb-i-Aqdas, p. 28*

"Economy is the foundation of human prosperity. The spendthrift is always in trouble. Prodigality on the part of any person is an unpardonable sin. We must never live on others like a parasitic plant.

Every person must have a profession, whether it be literary or manual, and must live a clean, manly, honest life, an example of purity to be imitated by others. It is more kingly to be satisfied with a crust of stale bread than to enjoy a sumptuous dinner of many courses, the money for which comes out of the pockets of others. The mind of a contented person is always peaceful and his heart at rest."

—*'Abdu'l-Bahá, Bahá'u'lláh and the New Era, p. 98*

BIBLIOGRAPHY

Advent of Divine Justice, The : Shoghi Effendi; India, New Delhi; Bahá'í Publishing Trust, 1968.

Auguste Forel and the Bahá'í Faith : Dr. Forel's letter to 'Abdu'l-Bahá and 'Abdu'l-Bahá's Tablet in reply—Translated from original German edition by George Ronald, Oxford; 1978.

Bahá'í World, The : An International record by Universal House of Justice; Haifa, Israel; 1974. Vol. IV, XI, XII.

Bahá'í World Faith : Selected Writings of Bahá'u'lláh and 'Abdu'l-Bahá. Wilmette, Illinois; Bahá'í Publishing Trust, 1943, 2nd edn. 1956, reprinted 1976.

Bahá'í Administration : Shoghi Effendi; Wilmette, Illinois; Bahá'í Publishing Trust, 1974.

Bahá'u'lláh and the New Era : J.E. Esslemont; London, Bahá'í Publishing Trust, 1923, 4th. edn. 1974.

Bahá'í Peace Program : Shoghi Effendi; Wilmette, Illinois; Published by National Spiritual Assembly of the United States and Canada; 1945.

Directives from the Guardian : India, New Delhi; Bahá'í Publishing Trust.

Foundation of World Unity : Compiled from Addresses and Tablets of 'Abdu'l-Bahá. Wilmette, Illinois; Bahá'í Publishing Committee,

2nd. edn. 1945.

God Passes By : Shoghi Effendi; Wilmette, Illinois; Bahá'í Publishing Trust, rev. edn. 1974, reprinted 1987.

Hidden Words, The : Bahá'u'lláh; translated by Shoghi Effendi, Germany; Bahá'í verlag, 1983.

Huqúqu'lláh : Compilation by the Research Department of the Universal House of Justice; India, New Delhi; Bahá'í Publishing Trust, 1974.

Lights of Guidance : Compilation by Helen Hornby; India, New Delhi; Bahá'í Publishing Trust, 1983.

Promised Day Is Come, The : Shoghi Effendi; India, New Delhi; Bahá'í Publishing Trust, 1976.

Principles of Bahá'í Administration : Compilation; U.K. Bahá'í Publishing Trust, 4th, edn. 1976; Indian rep. edn. 1982.

Promulgation of Universal Peace, The : Compilation; Wilmette, Illinois; Bahá'í Publishing Trust, 1982.

Portals to Freedom : By Howard Colby Ives; Oxford; George Ronald, 1953.

Paris Talks : Addresses by 'Abdu'l-Bahá; U.K., London; Bahá'í Publishing Trust, 11th, edn. 1969, rep. edn. 1979.

Renewal of Civilization, The : By David Hofman; India, New Delhi; Bahá'í Publishing Trust, 1969.

Star of the West : Oxford; George Ronald, Vol. XIII & VIII.

Some Answered Questions : 'Abdu'l-Bahá; India, New Delhi; Bahá'í Publishing Trust, 1973.

Secret of Divine Civilization : 'Abdu'l-Bahá; Wilmette, Illinois; Bahá'í Publishing Trust, 1975.

Synopsis and Codification of the Kitáb-i-Aqdas : Haifa; The Universal House of Justice, 1973.

Writings of Bahá'u'lláh : Compilation, National

Spiritual Assembly of the Bahá'ís of India. New Delhi; Bahá'í Publishing Trust, 1986.

World Order of Bahá'u'lláh, The : Shoghi Effendi; Wilmette, Illinois; Bahá'í Publishing Trust, 1965.

World Order Magazines : Wilmette, Illinois; Bahá'í Publishing Trust; Vol. XI, March 1946; Jan. 1949.